MAY 1 4 2018

DIGITAL AND INFORMATION LITERACY ™

ARTIFICIAL INTELLIGENCE

CLEVER COMPUTERS AND SMART MACHINES

JOE GREEK

rosen publishing's
rosen central®

New York

Published in 2018 by The Rosen Publishing Group, Inc.
29 East 21st Street, New York, NY 10010

Library of Congress Cataloging-in-Publication Data

Names: Greek, Joe, author.
Title: Artificial intelligence: clever computers and smart machines / Joe Greek.
Description: New York : Rosen Central, 2018. | Series: Digital and information literacy | Includes bibliographical references and index. | Audience: Grades 5–8.
Identifiers: LCCN 2017018775| ISBN 9781499438970 (library bound) | ISBN 9781499438956 (pbk.) | ISBN 9781499438963 (6 pack)
Subjects: LCSH: Artificial intelligence—Juvenile literature.
Classification: LCC TA347.A78 G74 2017 | DDC 006.3—dc23
LC record available at https://lccn.loc.gov/2017018775

Manufactured in China

CONTENTS

INTRODUCTION

In 2011, a shocking newcomer defeated two of the greatest contestants in the history of the television quiz show *Jeopardy*. Ken Jennings, who had the show's longest winning streak of seventy-four appearances, and fellow champion Brad Rutter had collectively earned more than $5 million in winnings during their appearances. The newcomer that defeated the two champions, however, was not even a person.

Instead, the victor was a powerful computer named Watson. Built by International Business Machines (IBM), Watson was what's known as a supercomputer. Supercomputers have a powerful ability to analyze vast amounts of data. Watson demonstrated to the world one example of a kind of advanced computer system known as artificial intelligence (AI).

AI refers to machines that carry out tasks—beyond merely physical ones—in ways that are human-like. In short, it is intelligence exhibited by machines, including computers and robots. The kind of AI that Watson uses is able to sift through data and use deductive reasoning to identify the correct answer to a question. Humans also use deductive reasoning to figure out the best answers or solutions to challenges.

Nearly every industry utilizes some type of AI system to perform tasks that help improve efficiency. At the same time, AI is increasingly making its way into everyday life at school, work, and home. With applications on

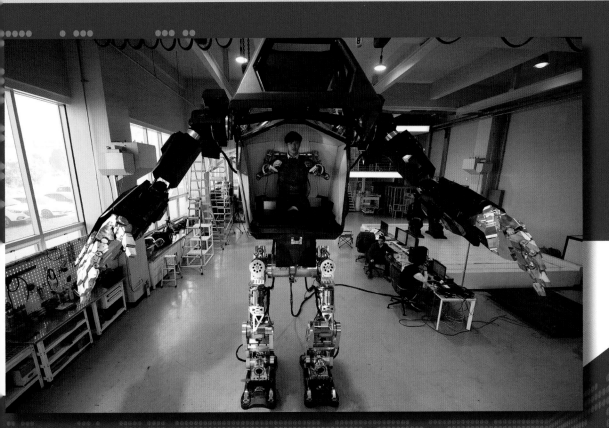

An engineer controls the 13-foot-tall (4 meter) Method-2 robot at the Hankook Mirae Technology labs in Gunpo, South Korea. Its robotic arms can hoist far more weight than a human ever could.

smartphones, tablets, and other devices, people often unknowingly use numerous AI systems throughout the day.

As AI systems start to come online, they will also change the way people live their lives. While AI's proponents hope to improve processes and work tasks, its widespread adoption will alter workforces around the world. Whereas human labor was once necessary for most tasks, AI, including AI-powered robots, is a likely future alternative. While there are issues with how AI might change society, and some even consider it threatening, many people remain excited about its possible applications.

The internet is another technology that needed several years of development before it became a staple of our work and personal lives. Even though AI research has existed for decades, the general public has not really seen it take off yet. Technology within this field of research, however, has grown exponentially and more companies are finding ways to develop products that utilize AI. In just a matter of years, AI could be more prevalent as it finds its way into more aspects of life.

Consider that a growing number of cars on the road today do not require an individual to operate the gas pedal or turn the steering wheel. In the future, many cars may be doing the driving while the passenger is just that—a passenger. AI development can provide humanity with an astounding number of opportunities. For a smooth and sustainable future, humans will have to wisely guide AI research and development for the betterment of people and society.

Chapter 1

From Fiction to Reality

When discussing AI, some people might imagine robots that exist alongside (or fight) people in science fiction thrillers. In reality, modern-day robots and their future iterations will probably differ greatly. Artificial Intelligence itself may diverge even more dramatically from the popular image that science fiction has created. Some people believe, for instance, that AI will exist mostly in the background—yet all around us—much as the internet has in the early twenty-first century. It is certainly possible that the AI of the future could be a giant, intelligence network, as well as individual computers and robots that exist and work among humanity.

Early Representations of AI

The idea that a comparable level of intelligence and self-awareness could exist outside of the human mind has been around for many centuries. One of the first-known depictions of AI arose in ancient Greek mythology. The story of Talos dates from 500 BCE and revolves around a giant automaton (a self-operating machine) made of bronze that protected the island of Crete. In one version of the story, Talos is said to have carried tablets with laws etched onto them throughout the island's villages. He would then act as a judge and settle disputes between the villagers.

Automatons can be considered the earliest real-life examples of robotics and of human attempts to create machines that can mimic human behavior. Unlike Talos, actual automatons lacked the power of formal reasoning. However, in many cases they were designed to resemble people, or other living creatures, in order to fool audiences. Automatons utilized a variety of engineering mechanisms, such as steam power and steel springs, to perform predetermined actions. Some early audiences may have been tricked into thinking the automatons had some kind of free will of their own.

Automatons are still produced to this day and are made for a variety of uses. Many decorative cuckoo clocks, for example, have miniature automatons that perform a set of functions at certain times of the day.

In addition to the physical aspects of human movement, thinkers have long tried to decode the secrets of formal reasoning as well. Gottfried Leibniz, a famous seventeenth-century mathematician and philosopher, speculated that formal reasoning could be broken down into a universal language or equation. In his theory, known as characteristic universalism, he proposed that our ability to reason between right or wrong could be illustrated in a formal language that everyone could understand. His theory is one of many that helped to lay the foundation for the study of AI in modern computer programming.

AI in Literature

Today's engineers and programmers have so far been unable to reproduce human intelligence. Nonetheless, you do not have to wait decades for science to catch up with our ambitions. A visit to your local library will undoubtedly yield a trove of literature that is chock-full of tales of AI. One of literature's most famous illustrations of man's attempt to recreate human intelligence is Mary Shelley's classic horror novel *Frankenstein*

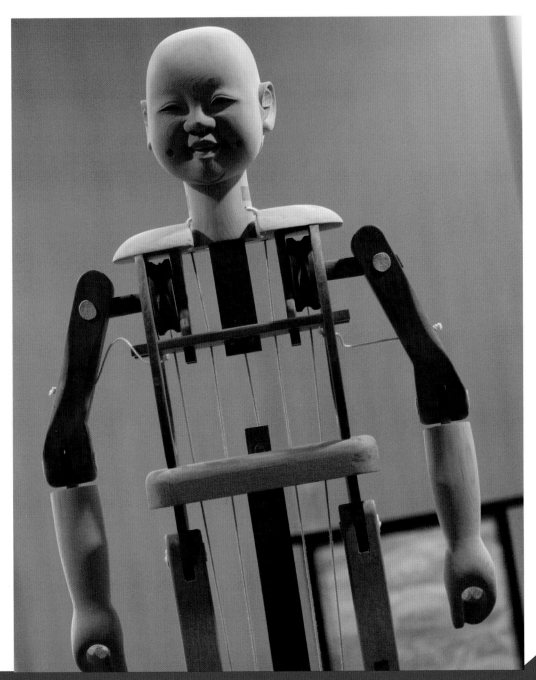

This is a replica of a Japanese mechanical Karakuri puppet that dates back to the seventeenth century. Such puppets were used as a form of entertainment both at home and in public performances.

File   Edit   View   Favorites   Tools   Help

ASIMOV'S THREE LAWS OF ROBOTICS

Asimov's Three Laws Of Robotics

Isaac Asimov is considered one of the great pioneers of science fiction. A prolific writer and imaginative storyteller, he wrote frequently on the subject of AI and its impact on society. Asimov's writings on AI and robotics were often focused on the potential threat they posed to humans. In an effort to protect his stories' characters, Asimov incorporated a fictional set of programming rules into the robots. These rules were intended to prevent them from causing harm.

1. A robot may not injure a human being or, through inaction, allow a human being to come to harm.
2. A robot must obey orders given it by human beings except where such orders would conflict with the First Law.
3. A robot must protect its own existence as long as such protection does not conflict with the First or Second Law.

As often was the case, the three laws could be subject to loopholes that had unintended consequences for his characters. Though Asimov was a writer of fiction, the future of AI may require safety standards similar to his three laws.

Isaac Asimov was one of the foremost science fiction authors of the twentieth century and often incorporated AI and robotics into his novels and stories.

(1818). In the novel, Dr. Frankenstein constructs a man from human and animal body parts and brings him to life. But the doctor ultimately is destroyed by his creation.

Classic science fiction authors of the mid-twentieth century, such as Isaac Asimov, Harlan Ellison, and Philip K. Dick, wrote about future societies—many of them in outer space—where human beings live alongside robots with comparable intelligence. Many of their stories examine the potential dangers of creating machines that are capable of making complex decisions without human help. Some of these warn that robots and machines would turn against us. Many such stories were also expressions of nineteenth- and twentieth-century social anxiety about an ever more mechanical and seemingly less human world that was ushered in by industry, bureaucracy, and other work environments.

In Ellison's *I Have No Mouth, and I Must Scream* (1967), self-aware AI destroy most of the human race through nuclear war. The potential harm that AI could cause to humans is not the only question that science fiction writers have dared to ask. Another major theme from science fiction that modern scientists and engineers take seriously is whether or not creating AI is ethical. In *Do Androids Dream of Electric Sheep?* (1968), Dick explored the notion of what it is to be human and whether or not a robot could truly possess self-awareness and empathy. In his dystopian future, readers were left to question whether or not a human-like soul could be simply produced in a factory and what that said about us as a people.

Chapter 2

The Development of AI

Many experts and thinkers who specialize in AI distinguish between two different types of AI. "Weak AI" refers to systems that can perform at a high level of intelligence, focusing on one narrow task or area of knowledge. In contrast, "strong AI" refers to a system that possesses a flexible and human-like level of intelligence. Strong AI systems aim to replicate a high level of intelligence across numerous areas of knowledge.

Goals of Artificial Intelligence

So far, strong AI has yet to be fully realized. Current versions of it do not come anywhere near the levels depicted in popular culture. Weak AI, on the other hand, has experienced a number of breakthroughs over the decades and has played an important role in the development of technology and society. AI applications can be spread out broadly across a variety of industries, and the list of fields affected by AI will only grow, so research goals vary accordingly. There are a few common goals that most AI researchers aim to meet:

- **Reasoning**: The ability to draw conclusions from available information is referred to as reasoning. For example, if an AI system were shown a key and a door, it would ideally figure out that the key should be used to unlock the door.
- **Planning**: To efficiently complete a task, an AI system needs to have the capacity to plan. Planning involves figuring out the steps necessary, and the order in which the steps should be done, to complete an overall task as quickly and efficiently as possible.
- **Learning**: Just as people learn from their mistakes and successes, one goal for creators of AI is to make a system that can learn from its previous actions and learn via trial and error.
- **Object Control**: Another goal of AI research is to develop systems that can safely and efficiently control an object. For example, a robot may one day be used to clean dishes or to wash and groom people's pets. The robot would need to be able to handle items without breaking or damaging them.

Though each AI system is designed for its own specific purposes, the primary objective for most researchers is to find ways to improve human life in some fashion. Weak AI systems can perform functions that people have previously been responsible for handling, which allows individuals to focus their expertise on tasks that AI simply cannot accomplish yet.

Turing, Strachey, and Oettinger

In the mid-twentieth century, the study of AI began to really take off. At this time, the first generations of computers were being developed and used by governments, universities, and research organizations. Though early computers were nowhere near as powerful as today's devices, they were able to calculate large amounts of data much faster than a person could by hand.

In 1950, British mathematician and computer pioneer Alan Turing predicted that machines eventually would be able to duplicate human intelligence. Turing devised a special test, eventually known as the Turing Test, which would determine if a machine or program possessed human-like intelligence. To conduct this test, a computer and a person, hidden from the view of a questioner, are given random identical questions. If the questioner is unable to distinguish the person from the machine by the answers, the machine is said to have passed the test. While there

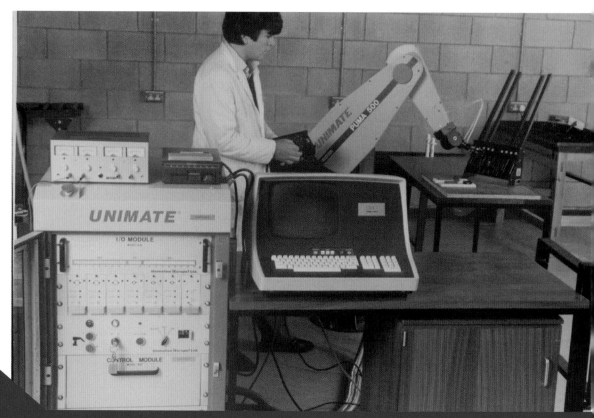

The Unimate Pumo 500 and Pumo 560 robots, shown here, were produced by Computer Integrated Manufacturing Systems (CMS) and helped to forever change industrial production.

have been disputed claims of programs beating the Turing Test, truly human-like AI has yet to be achieved.

The first successful AI program was created in 1951. Pioneering British computer scientist Christopher Strachey's checkers program was able to play an entire game of checkers, which was seen as a groundbreaking moment in computer and AI history.

Shortly after Strachey's breakthrough, Anthony Oettinger successfully developed a program that demonstrated an ability to learn on its own. In his program, simulated shopper would visit eight simulated shops looking for various items. With each visit, the program shopper would memorize a few items available at each shop. When ordered to grab a particular item, the program shopper remembered which shop had it and picked it up at the right store.

Development of Expert Systems

The 1960s brought about several developments in AI research, including expert systems. An expert system is a program that is designed to solve problems within a specific area of knowledge. Dendral, a program created at Stanford University in 1965, was the first expert system to be developed. It specialized in analyzing chemical compounds.

Expert systems consist of two primary parts: the knowledge base and the inference engine. Knowledge bases are essentially a collection of data, such as facts about a particular topic. Human experts compile the data within a knowledge base. The inference engine is a program that can scan the knowledge base and evaluate the data to provide a reliable solution to a problem or an answer to a question. The benefit of an expert system is that it can quickly scan and evaluate large volumes of data that would take a person much longer to do on their own. These programs have numerous commercial uses and are still used to this day. Many industries, such as the financial and medical industries, utilize expert systems to help professionals solve problems quickly and efficiently.

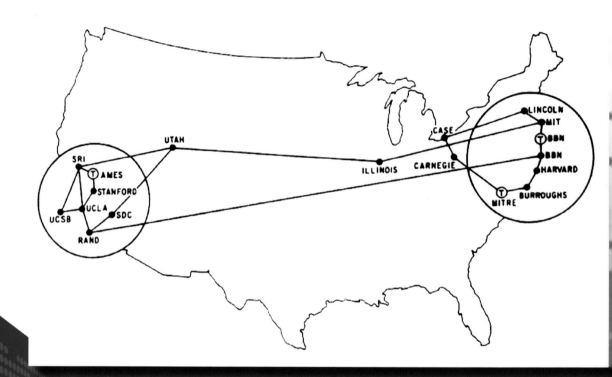

This map shows the 1972-era locations of communication centers and relays of the US Department of Defense's ARPANET (Advanced Research Projects Agency). This system was the predecessor of the modern internet.

As the internet found its way into more homes in the 1990s and 2000s, web developers found new uses for expert systems. Many online resources, such as WebMD's Symptom Checker, are built upon an expert system. Where as expert systems were once primarily used by universities and large companies that could afford the technology, ordinary people now have access to them at their fingertips.

MYTHS & FACTS

MYTH The research and development of AI aims to replace humans with machines.

FACT While breakthroughs in AI can lead to programs and machines that are able perform human tasks, there will always be a need for human experts. Progress in AI today and in the future will still require humans to initiate and control the development of the technology.

MYTH AI will eventually spin out of human control.

FACT Many science fiction stories warn of AI rebelling against its human masters and taking over the world. Researchers and developers actually take these concerns very seriously. AI systems will always be limited in the amount of data they can process. Unlike the human brain that can create new neural pathways, computer components can not change from their original state.

MYTH We are close to the development of a conscious AI system.

FACT Many breakthroughs have been made in AI research over the years. However, our knowledge of human consciousness remains incomplete, and will be incomplete for a long time. Building an AI system capable of independent thought and consciousness, if at all possible, is probably decades away.

17

Chapter 3

Modern AI

Advances and breakthroughs in AI research are occurring in labs throughout the world. In past decades, researchers and engineers did not lack the ambition and talent to create AI systems. But other priorities took precedence, including conventional military technologies, biotechnology, and other pursuits. In addition, truly advanced AI has only become a possibility with advanced microchip technologies that have accompanied the personal computing revolution.

Today, much of the research in AI happens at universities, in government labs, and within the private sector. Part of the reason that AI technology has exploded in popularity in recent years is because companies are finding more uses for the technology that directly benefit or impact everyday people. Many of these uses might also be profitable—for consumers, governments, and even the military.

More Than a Game of Chess

To succeed at chess, players need to examine a variety of potential moves and their outcomes before making a series of decisions. At the highest, championship levels, chess requires great intelligence and instinct. As a result, few AI breakthroughs are held in as high esteem as the victory of IBM's Deep Blue computer over international chess world champion Garry Kasparov.

Deep Blue's development began in 1985 when Feng Suing Hsu, a Carnegie Mellon University student, began building a chess-playing computer named ChipTest. After Thomas Anantharaman and Murray Campbell joined the project, the computer became known as Deep Thought. After news of the project spread, IBM hired the team to continue research and development, with state-of-the-art labs now at their disposal.

World chess champion Garry Kasparov thinks very carefully about his next move in his second of two appearances playing against the IBM Deep Blue computer, in New York City in 1997.

In 1989, Russian chess master Garry Kasparov easily beat Deep Thought in a two-game match. Undeterred, the team continued their research and renamed their computer Deep Blue—a combination of Deep Thought and IBM's nickname, Big Blue. In 1996, Kasparov faced off against Deep Blue for a six-game match. Though Deep Blue could examine 100 million chess positions per second, Kasparov ultimately won 4-2.

By 1997, the IBM team had enhanced Deep Blue's calculating ability to examine 200 million different positions per second. This technological leap gave Deep Blue the edge it needed to defeat Kasparov. On May 11 of that year, Deep Blue won the final match, resulting in a 3.5 to 2.5 overall victory. Kasparov, upset that he lost to a machine, stormed off the stage.

File   Edit   View   Favorites   Tools   Help

MOORE'S LAW

Moore's Law

In 1965, Gordon Moore observed that as computer technology advanced each year, the number of transistors per square inch on integrated circuits doubled. His observation showed that technology grows at an exponential rate while the resources required to make the tech and energy required to power it decline. Consider how early computers took up entire floors of buildings. Today, hand-held smartphones are more powerful than most home computers of the 1990s. Moore later cofounded Intel, and his observation became known as Moore's Law. This rule of thumb suggests that in just twenty years' time, we could be looking at much more advanced AI systems, perhaps even ones that rival the complex pathways of the human brain.

Deep Blue's victory was a major milestone in AI development. Nonetheless, Deep Blue should not be categorized as a strong AI; it focused on just one specific task—beating Kasparov.

Supercomputers of Vast Knowledge

Deep Blue was not a typical computer; it was a specialized machine known as a supercomputer. At the time it was built, supercomputers were the most powerful class of computers in the world.

One of the factors that distinguishes a supercomputer from a conventional computer is that it has more than one central processing unit (CPU). A CPU is the primary component of a computer, which acts as the machine's brain by calculating and interpreting data. Early supercomputers contained only a few CPUs. These machines were still capable of processing much larger volumes of data then a human being could process. In fact, a great number of human experts working on the same data would be required to even come close to matching a supercomputer's processing speed.

IBM's Naval Ordnance Research Calculator (NORC) is generally considered the first supercomputer. This particular machine was in service from 1954 to 1963 and was used to calculate missile trajectories. The development of NORC and the rise of supercomputing coincided with the Cold War. This decades-long period was marked by great tensions between the United States and the former Soviet Union, which became modern-day Russia. The potential for a full-blown war led to major government investment in supercomputers and artificial intelligence.

By the 1990s, the price of supercomputers had declined and businesses began to show interest in these tools. In previous decades supercomputers had contained only a few CPUs, but by the 1990s these machines contained thousands of them. To this day, supercomputers are used in a variety of industries for market research and to improve business practices. And militaries are among the most prolific users of supercomputers. Countries around the world still race year after year to build the biggest and smartest computers.

The Cray-1 was a supercomputer released by Cray Research and first installed in 1976 at Los Alamos National Laboratory in New Mexico. It went on to become one of the most commercially successful ones of its time, selling 80 units for up to $10 million apiece.

AI in the Cloud

Today, the "cloud" is an important resource for new technology. A lot of the data and software that we access online is stored on the internet rather than the hard drive of your device. You can think of this information as existing in a cloud of lots of other information on the internet; this is how the cloud got its name. When someone watches a movie on Netflix, for example, they are accessing data in the cloud.

There is a growing trend among the individuals and businesses to utilize cloud technologies. Cloud-based information can be accessed from any location that has an internet connection. This makes it convenient for people who travel a lot or for groups of people who need to work together on the same projects.

Many developers believe that cloud computing has made a big shift in AI research and development. Essentially, the cloud makes it possible for individuals to access the power of a supercomputer without having to physically have one. This development also opens the door for more people and businesses to utilize supercomputers and AI programs, which would have cost hundreds of thousands, if not millions, of dollars in the past. Many AI-like systems within the cloud are free and are already used by the general public. Google, for example, provides free access to systems that can translate foreign languages and identify images. As browsers become ever more intuitive and the software connected to them becomes ever more sophisticated, the foundation for future AI efforts grows ever more solid and welcoming

The Rise of Automation

As technology, including robotics and AI, has improved over the decades, we have also seeing a rise in automation. Automation is the ability of machinery or equipment to operate automatically, with little or no human control. This ability to self-regulate enables machines to perform tasks that were ordinarily carried out by humans. While basic automation has existed for centuries, AI systems allow machines to perform ever more complicated and subtle tasks.

One common example of automation is the automated teller machine (ATM). ATMs can perform a variety of common tasks that employees at a bank to perform in the past. Powered by a computer and internet connection, ATMs allow people to withdraw and deposit money and check balances on their bank accounts, all without having to wait for a bank

Many technologists believe that remote servers powering cloud technology could help the acceleration of AI development. Here, a worker maintains servers at Facebook's Prinvelle Data Center in Prineville, Oregon.

employee. These machines can be found all over the map, including at gas stations, grocery stores, and shopping centers.

One example of automated machinery currently utilizing more advanced AI systems is the self-driving car. Engineers have experimented with automated vehicles since the early twentieth century, but the first truly autonomous vehicles were built in the 1980s by Carnegie Mellon University.

Until recently, only engineers, scientists, and automotive researchers had access to self-driving technologies. However, many cars on the market today, including those made by Tesla, Inc., have varying degrees of autonomous capabilities—or at least future potential for them. Tesla's

Model 3, for example, is equipped with full self-driving hardware. While self-driving vehicles are still limited by law, this hardware will allow the Model 3, and all other Tesla vehicles, to convert to full self-driving capabilities in the near future.

Factories and distribution centers are also seeing an increase in automation. Online retailer Amazon owns numerous facilities where robots drive though vast warehouses to pick up products that have been ordered by customers.

German automaker Volkswagen revealed a protoype for a self-driving car in 2017 called Cedric, shown here at the Geneva International Motor Show in Geneva, Switzerland.

Manufacturers, such as automakers, also utilize robots on their assembly and production lines. These machines build parts that were once put together by people.

Although the automation breakthroughs we have discussed exemplify a high level of complexity and ingenuity, they are still considered weak AI systems, rather than strong. Nonetheless, applications associated with automation and AI are drastically changing industries around the world and research indicates that even bigger changes are on the horizon.

Chapter 4

Redesigning Society

The continued development of AI will likely play a big role in the evolution of human society and civilization. It has already had an impact in how contemporary people live. Note, again, that with the advent of the internet, online hyperconnectedness is the norm in most Western societies now—a huge change from merely fifteen years ago. As mankind attempts to predict the future five, ten, and even fifty years out, AI's influence in daily life could grow exponentially.

The Power of AI Already at Your Fingertips

Already, advanced AI-like systems have found their way into hands of millions of people. You might not think it, but many of the smartphones and tablets that people use on a daily basis are equipped with varying degrees of AI technology.

In 2011, Apple unveiled its intelligent personal assistant application, known as Siri. Siri utilizes voice recognition software to help users with a number of tasks. For instance, a user can ask Siri to look up directions, find

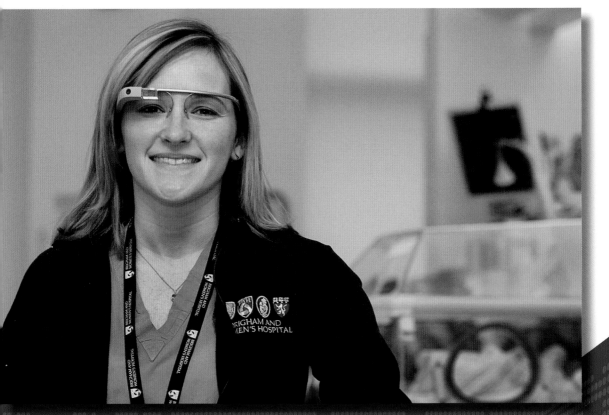

Existing technologies, such as Google Glass, shown here being worn by a hospital nurse, may inform new developments in AI, including serving as new models for future robots' visual sensorary inputs.

a recipe, or add an event to a calendar. Other smartphone and device makers have their own versions of Siri, as well as a catalogue of AI-based applications that perform different functions.

Another type of consumer device that utilizes AI systems is optical-display mounted headgear, such as Google Glass. These types of devices essentially overlay a computer display on the user's field of vision. These devices have many potential applications, some of which may improve people's lives. The Autism Glass Project, for example, is attempting to develop a program that use AI technology to recognize people's faces and facial expressions. Intended for individuals with autism who often have difficulty interpreting facial expressions, the program aims to provide real-time analysis of what the user is seeing.

On the Road and at Home

In the future, AI has the potential to completely transform the way we live our everyday lives. We've already discussed driverless vehicles in previous sections, but the overall impact they may have on society could be huge. According to Stanford University's "One Hundred Year Study on Artificial Intelligence," by 2030 driverless vehicles will be widely adopted by the public. The study suggests that the reliability and safety of this technology will encourage people to move outside of cities, which will change human population distribution.

Autonomous robotic vacuum cleaners were first commercially introduced in the early 2000s and are the first example of a physical robot or AI-related system becoming popular in households.

Life at home may also be radically changed as more technologies with AI capabilities are developed. Already, many homes are equipped with autonomous vacuum cleaners that are pre-programming to routinely clean a house. Future households will see an increasing number of internet-connected AI technologies that communicate with each other to carry out a variety of tasks, including security, energy, and home goods management. For example, refrigerators are being developed that can identify when certain foods have been consumed. When a product is depleted, the refrigerator can notify the homeowner to re-up on the goods, or even automatically purchase them online and have them delivered. The promise of AI is that it will give people a reprieve from the drudgery and hassle of repetitive tasks.

Changing the Landscape of Health Care

AI systems are also on the verge of changing the health care industry. Today, there are already smartphone applications that track heart rates and physical activity to help people improve their exercise routines. The future, however, could see systems that efficiently tie together patient readings and data to make decisions on care. AI systems might also be able to scan vast databases of patients to identify common traits and trends. This could usher in a era of very fine-tuned and more accurate diagnoses.

Using AI may free up medical staff from physical labor for tasks that include cleaning and managing patient records. AI will not necessarily replace experts within the industry anytime soon, but they will provide support to those individuals and teams. That additional support they will provide to human experts will allow patients to receive more customized direct care from their physicians that are often challenged by understaffing amid large numbers of patients. In the far future, however, robots may become skilled enough to handle complicated operations, such as neurosurgery. Still, it will take a good amount of time and research before the general public is comfortable enough to allow robots to carry out such delicate procedures.

— ☐ X

File   Edit   View   Favorites   Tools   Help

     TECHNOLOGY ON THE BATTLEFIELD

Technology on the Battlefield

Currently, militaries around the world use AI systems for aerial and ground drones. These machines survey enemy strongholds and territory, and help deliver deadly airstrikes. The US Department of Defense (DOD) is focusing on AI that can be used in robotic fighter jets, bombers, and other aircraft. Other military branches are looking into marine vehicles guided by AI. Reminiscent of the 1980s sci-fi thriller The Terminator and its sequels, wars of the future may be executed largely by machines. Of course, the moral issues arising from mechanized warfare are complicated. Removing soldiers from harm's way does not make for bloodless conflict, if you consider the many civilians and innocent people often caught in a war's crossfire. In addition, remote operators guiding drones in war zones from thousands of miles away still suffer from post-traumatic stress disorder (PTSD), much like combat veterans do.

Two US Navy seamen troubleshoot a drone on the USS *Mesa Verde* at sea in the Atlantic Ocean as part of a training exercise.

A Job Destroyer or Creator?

As AI becomes more prominent in our daily lives, many people are worried that the technology will take away jobs from millions of people, further hurting a working class already in trouble from the automation of the twentieth century. Manufacturing jobs already declined as machines become more efficient. AI is likely to infiltrate into nearly every industry in which people are currently the primary source of labor force.

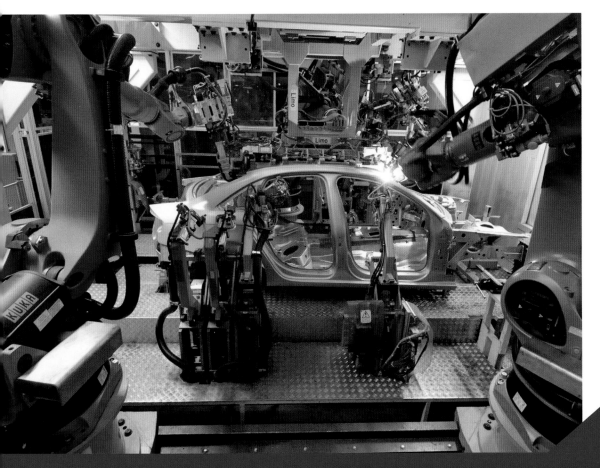

Robotic systems help assemble an Audi automobile in a factory in Ingolstadt, Bavaria, Germany. Factories may one day function with barely any people at all.

AI could cause widespread job losses for workers. Even if changes are gradual, over time AI could have serious social consequences. In the last few decades, manufacturing jobs in the United States and other industrial nations have declined and have been replaced only with lower paid service sector jobs. This has been devastating for many communities. What happens when AI and robots begin to put even service workers—like employees in retail and food service—out of work? It will be a huge challenge for govern-ment, individuals, researchers, and academics to figure out ways to lessen these shocks.

Conversely, AI could also generate new jobs and entirely new indus-tries. Humans will always be needed to guide these efforts. AI was derived from centuries of human imagination and will continue to be developed in support of humanity, rather than against it. In the end, humans will continue to dream up new areas of technology and research, in which that AI will play a supporting role

Chapter 5

Planning for a Future Career in AI

There is no single career in AI because it is consists of several different areas of expertise. As you begin planning a career path in AI, you will want to consider which areas interest you the most. The great thing about this field is that the opportunities are potentially endless, as its fascinating potential applications continue to expand.

Computer science is the most basic foundation of all AI research and development. Most industries utilize internal computer systems and internet technologies. AI-focused projects can be some of the most challenging and exciting available to those interested in this field of study. Programming is at the heart of most of the computer science that helps run the internet and its connected devices. Just like complex video games and cinematic special effects require many lines of code, AI is a labor-intensive and competitive field for savvy code specialists.

Predictive Analytics and Machine Learning

One prerequisite for building an AI capable of learning is getting acquainted with predictive analytics. This branch of research focuses heavily on building programs that can make predictions about the future. Predictive analytics identify patterns within data to make educated guesses on what occurs after certain actions are taken. To make these educated guesses, it relies heavily on the ability of the program to learn from past actions.

In order to work in this particular segment of AI research and development, one must usually obtain a college degree in computer science. Individuals interested in this career path will generally find jobs creating computer programs that rely heavily on data and complicated algorithms. Many companies, including social media networks, utilize predictive analytics to create programs that interact with real people. One example of a predictive analytics in the real world is a customer service chat program on a website that asks users a series of questions to identify a solution to a question or problem.

Natural Language Processing and Computer Vision

Certain AI sectors aim to improve human interactions. Consequently, experts in natural language processing (NLP) and computer vision are needed. As with predictive analytics and machine learning, these careers generally require computer science degrees. NLP has helped break language barriers among internet-connected people worldwide. Google Translate, for example, is a free NLP program that can translate speech from numerous languages. While many breakthroughs have occurred in NLP and computer vision research, there is still plenty of work to do in order to perfect these systems. They will ultimately play an important role in robotic engineering as future machines dominate homes and workplaces.

Robotic Engineering

While computer programming makes the brains behind AI, robotic engineering concerns itself with the body. A career in robotic engineering starts with a

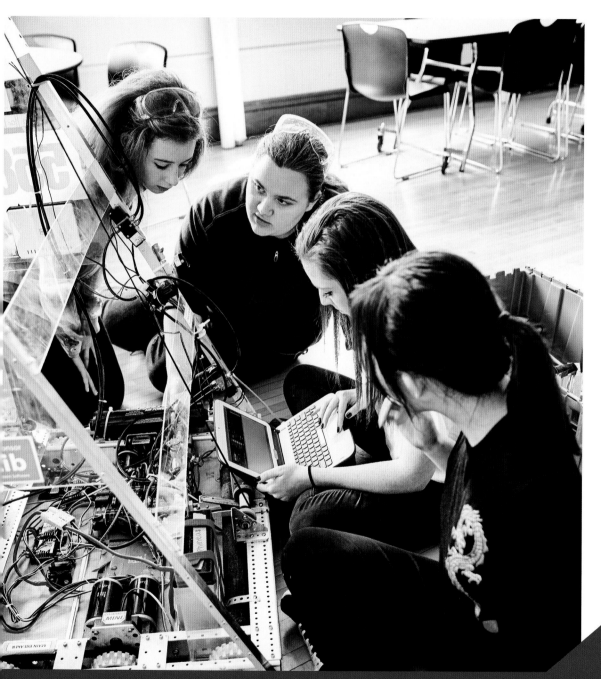

These high schoolers worked together to build and program a functional robot. In recent years, there has been an explosion of interest in robotics in the form of clubs, coursework, and other activities.

Massachustts Institute of Technology (MIT) professor Cynthia Breazeal stands in front of Kismet, a humanoid robot that was designed to interact with people by reacting to vocal and physical expressions.

degree in electrical or mechanical engineering, often with a focus on robotics. Engineers design and test robots that can be used for a variety of applications, including manufacturing and military uses. Engineers generally do most of their work with computer-aided design software. Computer models can simulate robot functionality before funding is obtained and labor is employed to produce

The National Aeronautics and Space Administration (NASA) built this robot, Val, which walks slowly in front of a group of students at the University of Massachusetts-Lowell robotics center.

the actual machines. Robotic engineers must be knowledgeable in electronic wiring and configuration and know how to connect the various components that make up the entire machine. If strong AI progresses, robotic engineers be able to construct actual androids similar to those depicted in science fiction.

College and Beyond

Most jobs in AI will require college- and graduate-level degrees. Some companies or AI sectors may even require specific course work in AI.

Young enthusiasts get advice on radio assembly from adults at the Mt. Elliott Makerspace in Detroit, Michigan, which is held in a church basement in an economically disenfranchised neighborhood.

Professions in AI will likely come to be incorporated every industry. Governments are generally the largest funders of AI research and often partner with universities, making future jobs in these sectors a safe bet. AI research for defense, health care, and other societal needs will likely provide lifelong career paths for students ready to put in the work.

Building a career in AI, however, doesn't have to wait until college. Students can begin preparing for the rigors of research and development by focusing heavily on mathematics, science, engineering, and computer courses in high school. Meanwhile, it is recommended that students research AI and decide whether this is the specific sector of STEM—science, technology, engineering, and math—in which they want to pursue opportunities.

TEN GREAT QUESTIONS

TO ASK AN AI ENGINEER

1   What area of AI research do you work in?

2   What college degrees or other educational degrees do you have?

3   What are the biggest challenges with your job?

4   What do you like the most and least about your job?

5   What types of projects have you worked on?

6   What programs do you use most in your job?

7   What will be the next breakthrough in AI technology?

8   Which industries are utilizing AI the most?

9   Would you suggest doing an internship?

10   What advice would you give to your younger self?

GLOSSARY

analytics Information that is produced by a computer program that analyzes data or statistics.

autism A disorder that is generally characterized by problems with interpersonal interaction and communication and sometimes marked by obsessive or repetitive behaviors.

autonomous To exist or function independent of anything else.

breakthrough A sudden advance in knowledge or technology.

consciousness The state of being aware of one's existence and the ability to engage in independent thought.

data In computing, any information or content, usually transmitted in the form of numeric code over the internet's infrastructure.

ethical Adhering to clearly defined standards of right and wrong in particular contexts.

industry A grouping of businesses that provide a particular product or service.

mythology Fictional stories that often focus on the deities and heroes of a particular group of people.

proliferation The act of something increasing in number at a rapid pace.

revolutionize To change drastically or completely a process or system that had been generally accepted as the standard.

transistor An electronic device that is used to control the flow of electricity in electronic equipment such as a computer.

FOR MORE INFORMATION

Allen Institute for Artificial Intelligence
2157 North Northlake Way, Suite 110
Seattle, WA 98103
(206) 548-5600
Website: http://www.allenai.org
Facebook: @AllenInstuteForAI
Twitter: @AllenAI_Org
This organization was created by Microsoft cofounder Paul Allen with the
    goal of conducting AI research and engineering and an emphasis on
    scientific and medical research.

Association for the Advancement of Artificial Intelligence (AAAI)
2275 East Bayshore Road, Suite 160
Palo Alto, CA 94303
(650) 328-3123
Website: http://www.aaai.org
Twitter: @RealAAAI
The AAAI is a nonprofit scientific society that aims to advance the under-
    standing of AI. The group also strives to promote an ethical approach
    to research and development of AI.

Canadian Artificial Intelligence Association (CAIAC)
Website: https://www.caiac.ca
CAIAC's mission is to promote research, development, and education in
    Canada's AI community through the sharing of knowledge. The group
    brings together professionals within Canada's AI research and devel-
    opment industry by hosting events and competitions.

Computing Research Association (CRA)
1828 L Street NW, Suite 800
Washington, DC 20036-4632
(202) 234-2111
Website: http://www.cra.org
Facebook: @ComputingResearch
Twitter: @CRATweets
YouTube: @ComputingResearch
The CRA's mission is to promote innovation in technology by bringing together professionals from industry, government, and academia. The group aims to increase the understanding of computing research by promoting awareness with lawmakers and the general public.

Machine Intelligence Research Institute (MIRI)
2030 Addision Street, 7th Floor
Berkeley, CA 94704
Website: https://intelligence.org
Facebook: @MachineIntelligenceResearchInstitute
Twitter: @MIRIBerkeley
MIRI is a nonprofit group that strives to increase the knowledge of mathematics that underlies the structure of intelligent behavior. The organization's mission is to help build safer and more reliable AI systems.

Websites

Because of the changing nature of internet links, Rosen Publishing has developed an online list of websites related to the subject of this book. This site is updated regularly. Please use this link to access this list:

http://www.rosenlinks.com/DIL/AI

FOR FURTHER READING

Behnam, Salemi. *Robot Building for Teens*. Independence, KY: Cengage Learning, 2014.

Berlatsky, Noah. *Artificial Intelligence* (Opposing Viewpoints). Farmington Hills, MI: Greenhaven Press, 2011.

Ceceri, Kathy. *Making Simple Robots: Exploring Cutting-Edge Robotics with Everyday Stuff*. San Francisco, CA: Maker Media, 2015.

Ceceri, Kathy. *Robotics: Discover The Science and Technology of the Future with 20 Projects* (Build It Yourself). White River Junction, VT: Nomad Press, 2012.

Flasinski, Mariusz. *Introduction to Artificial Intelligence*. New York, NY: Springer Publishing, 2016.

Freedman, Jeri. *Robots Through History* (Robotics). New York, NY: Rosen Central, 2011.

George, Dr. Binto, and Gail Carmichael. *Artificial Intelligence Simplified: Understanding Basic Concepts*. Bettendorf, IA: CSTrends LLP, 2016.

Kasparov, Garry. *Deep Thinking: Where Machine Intelligence Ends and Human Creativity Begins*. New York, NY: Hachette Book Group, 2017.

Niver, Heather. *Careers for Tech Girls in Computer Science* (Tech Girls). New York, NY: Rosen Publishing Inc., 2016.

Ryan, Peter. *Powering Up a Career in Robotics* (Preparing for Tomorrow's Careers). New York, NY: Rosen Publishing Inc., 2016.

Winter, Max. *Powering Up a Career in Artificial Intelligence* (Preparing for Tomorrow's Careers). New York, NY: Rosen Publishing Inc., 2016.

BIBLIOGRAPHY

Bell, Lee. "What Is Moore's Law? WIRED Explains the Theory That Defined the Tech Industry." *Wired*, August 28, 2016. http://www.wired.co.uk/article/wired-explains-moores-law.

Best, Jo. "IBM Watson: The Inside Story of How the Jeopardy-winning Supercomputer was Born and What it Wants to do Next." TechRepublic, September 9, 2013. http://www.techrepublic.com/articleibm-watson-the-inside-story-of-how-the-jeopardy-winning-super-computer-was-born-and-what-it-wants-to-do-next.

Goodwins, Rupert. "Debunking the Biggest Myths About Artificial Intelligence." Ars Technica, December 25, 2015. https://arstechnica.com/information-technology/2015/12/demystifying-artificial-intelligence-no-the-singularity-is-not-just-around-the-corner.

Ha, Thu-Huong. "Researchers Want to Use Google Glass to Help Autistic People 'See' Emotions." Quartz, October 21, 2015. https://qz.com/528840/researchers-want-to-use-google-glass-to-help-autistic-people-see-emotions.

Lewis, Tanya. "A Brief History of Artificial Intelligence." LiveScience, December 4, 2014. http://www.livescience.com/49007-history-of-artificial-intelligence.html.

Maney, Kevin. "How Artificial Intelligence and Robots Will Radically Transform the Economy." *Newsweek*, November 30, 2016. http://www.newsweek.com/2016/12/09/robot-economy-artificial-intelligence-jobs-happy-ending-526467.html.

Markoff, John, and Matthew Rosenberg. "The Pentagon's 'Terminator Conundrum': Robots That Would Kill on Their Own." *New York Times*, October 25, 2016. https://www.nytimes.com/2016/10/26/us/pentagon-artificial-intelligence-terminator.html.

Matlis, Jan. "A Brief History of Supercomputers." *Computerworld*, May 31, 2005. http://www.computerworld.com.au/article/132504/ brief_history_supercomputers.

Metz, Cade. "Google Is Sharing Its Powerful AI with Everyone in Its Cloud." *Wired*, March 23, 2016. https://www.wired.com/2016/03/ google-sharing-powerful-ai-everyone-cloud.

Newman, Daniel. "Why IoT Will Give Rise to Artificial Intelligence." *Forbes*, August 11, 2016. https://www.forbes.com/sites/danielnew- man/2016/08/11/why-iot-will-give-rise-to-artificial-intelligence/ #d44f909602ce.

Simonite, Tom. "2014 in Computing: Breakthroughs in Artificial Intelligence." MIT Technology Review, December 29, 2014. https://www.technologyreview.com/s/533686/2014-in-computing- breakthroughs-in-artificial-intelligence.

Stone, Peter, et al. "Artificial Intelligence and Life in 2030." One Hundred Year Study on Artificial Intelligence: Report of the 2015-2016 Study Panel. Stanford University, Stanford, CA, September 2016. https://ai100.stanford.edu/2016-report.

Trckova-Flamee, Dr. Alena. "Talos." *MMIX Encyclopedia Mythica*, March 3, 1997. http://www.pantheon.org/articles/t/talos.html.

Walter, Damien. "When AI Rules the World: What SF Novels Tell Us About Our Future Overlords." *Guardian*, March 18, 2016. https://www. theguardian.com/books/booksblog/2016/mar/18/ai-sf-novels- artificial-intelligence-science-fiction-gibson-neuromancer.

INDEX

About the Author

With a background in journalism, Joe Greek has written on a variety of topics pertaining to technology and its impact on society. Some of his past titles in the Digital and Information Literacy series include *Social Activism Online: Getting Involved* and *Incredible Projects Using 3D Printing*.

Photo Credits